Easy Master Themes
Level One

Arrangements of Themes by Ten Master Composers

Compiled and Edited by Jeff Schaum

FOREWORD

This series helps to widen the student's musical horizons by offering an introduction of some of the world's greatest music. These arrangements enable a pupil to have the satisfaction of hands on experience with master themes, after only a few months study. Music appreciation benefit is provided by a biography and portrait of each composer. Selections include orchestral, ballet, opera, operetta and piano literature.

A brief music dictionary is found on page 24.

INDEX

SCHAUM PUBLICATIONS, INC.
10235 N. Port Washington Rd. - Mequon, WI 53092
www.schaumpiano.net

07-26
JE-2

Wolfgang Amadeus Mozart

(MOE-tsart) 1756-1791

Mozart's father was a gifted German composer and violin player, and he quickly recognized the gifts for music Wolfgang and his sister Maria had. The Mozarts embarked on tours of Europe playing for nobility and receiving rave reviews. The pace of touring during his early years weakened Mozart's frail constitution, thus contributing to his early death at age 35.

Despite his short life, Mozart composed an amazing amount of music, including 41 symphonies. Mozart continued to refine the form of the symphony started by Haydn. Symphonies No. 40 and 41 (Jupiter) were composed during the summer of 1788 and are considered his finest. Mozart's orchestras were somewhat larger than those in Haydn's day, and Mozart was a master at getting beautiful contrasts in tone color from the orchestra.

J.B. Cramer, a famous music critic of the time, added the nickname "Jupiter" to Symphony 41 because of the "loftiness and nobility of the music."

Duet Accompaniment

In the accompaniments, notes with *stems up* are to be played with the *right hand*. Notes with *stems down* are to be played with the *left hand*.

Symphony No. 41

(3rd mvt. theme)

Wolfgang Amadeus Mozart

Moderato

Nikolay Rimsky-Korsakov

(RIM-skee CORE-sah-kov) 1844-1908

Rimsky-Korsakov started his musical career as a child, by taking piano lessons. He continued lessons throughout school and took a few years off to enter the Naval Academy in St. Petersburg. After his enlistment was over, he returned to St. Petersburg where he continued studying composition.

He was one of the greatest masters of Russian music, and *Scheherazade* reflects his use of Russian melodies, rhythms and tone colors. Modern music scholars consider Rimsky-Korsakov one of the best orchestrators of all time.

Scheherazade is a ballet that tells the tales of the Arabian Nights. One of the stories is about a jealous sultan who thinks his wife is cheating on him. He pretends to go on a hunting expedition, but returns suddenly to check up on his wife. To his surprise, he walks in on a wild party that has been going on in his absence. Tragic events and death follow, bringing the story to an unhappy ending.

Duet Accompaniment

Scheherazade

L.H. Position

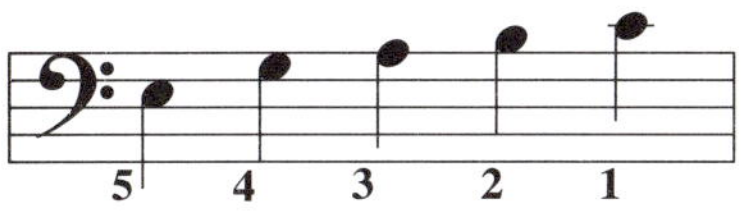

R.H. Position

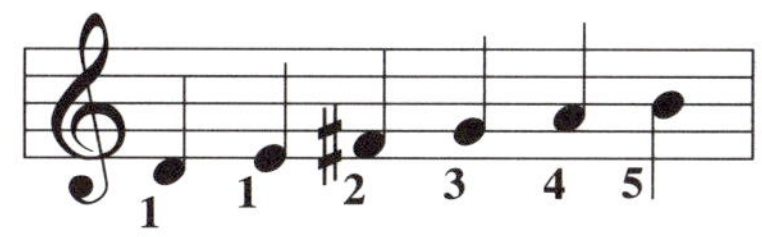

Andantino

Nikolay Rimsky-Korsakov

Cesar Franck

(FRAHNK) 1822-1890

Belgium born Cesar Franck was a child prodigy who spent most of his life in France. He won a singing contest at age nine and a piano contest at age twelve. After entering the Paris conservatory, he continued capturing awards for his piano and organ playing, for his excellent work in counterpoint and for his fugues.

After leaving the conservatory Franck devoted himself almost exclusively to organ playing and teaching. He was extremely influential on the next generation of French composers.

Franck did not write a lot of music, but what he did write was of the highest quality. His symphony was finished in 1888, when he was 66 years old. His symphony was the first to use an English horn in the orchestra.

Duet Accompaniment

Symphony in D Minor

(1st mvt. theme)

L.H. Position

R.H. Position

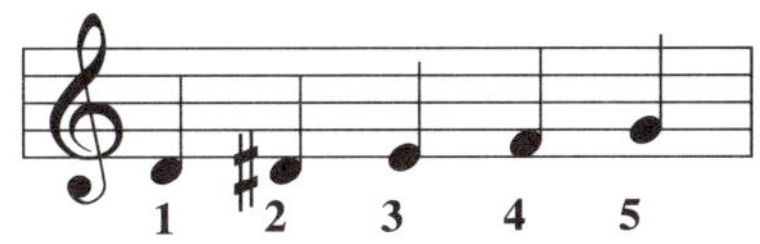

Lento

Cesar Franck

Amilcare Ponchielli

(pahn-key-ELL-lee) 1834-1886

Ponchielli studied music from his shopkeeper / organist father at his village church and was able to enter the Milan conservatory at age nine. By age ten he had already composed a symphony. After his studies he became a church organist and director of the municipal bands in Piacenza and Cremona and also began composing music for opera. He eventually became professor of composition at the Milan conservatory and wrote operas, cantatas, ballets, instrumental and vocal chamber music. Music historians consider him the most important Italian opera composer besides Verdi in the late 19th century.

This melody is from his ballet *La Gioconda*. In the story a beautiful street singer spurns the attentions of a spy, so the spy accuses her mother of being a witch. The mother is eventually saved and there is a great dance (Dance of the Hours) that marks the triumph of good over evil.

Duet Accompaniment

Dance of the Hours

Amilcare Ponchielli

Allegro

Johann Sebastian Bach

(BAHKH) 1685-1750

The name Bach is synonymous with music. Johann Sebastian was the most famous of a large family of German musicians. Bach married twice, and between his two wives had more than twenty children, though only ten survived past childhood. Although Bach was an outstanding organist, he was also an excellent Latin teacher. He is recognized as musical genius. Serious musicians since his time have studied his pieces to find out the "correct" way to do things.

Bach spent most of his life as a teacher and composer of works designed for immediate performance in the classroom and church. Even though an enormous amount of Bach's music has survived, some historians estimate that about half of Bach's total output has been lost. No single musician has been more influential and remained as popular to this day as Johann Sebastian Bach.

Duet Accompaniment

Minuet

(from the piano book of Anna Magdalena Bach)

L.H. Positions

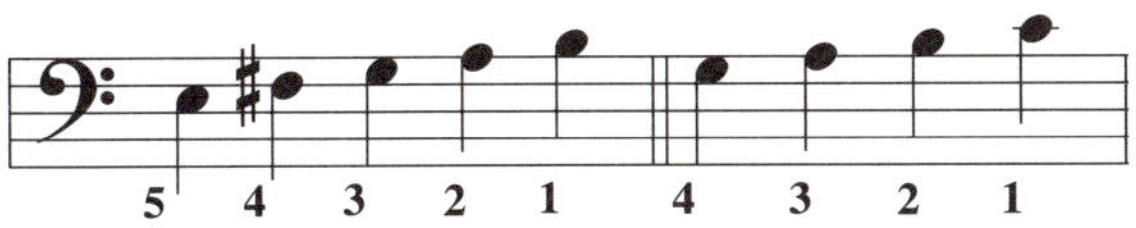

R.H. Positions

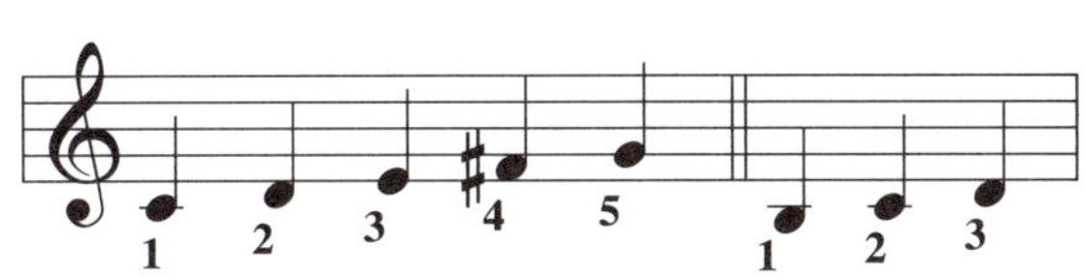

Andante

Johann Sebastian Bach

Franz Joseph Haydn

(HIGH-den) 1732-1809

Haydn was the second of twelve children, and grew up in Germany in a house that his mother insisted be kept neat and tidy - and expected her children to help keep it that way. Haydn was an excellent singer as a child, and was a star choirboy. He received much of his musical training while he was a choirboy, and shortly thereafter began composing music of his own. Although Haydn's parents wanted him to go into the priesthood, he resisted their pressures and focused on music. At first, Haydn struggled to make a living at music. He stayed with it, and eventually was appointed court composer by Prince Esterhazy, where he remained for nearly 30 years.

Nicknamed "Papa Haydn," he was known as the father of the symphony, and in all wrote 108 symphonies. He was very influential in the establishment of the classical style, and he helped popularize both string quartets and oratorios.

This piece is from the second movement of Symphony No. 94 - called the "Surprise" symphony because of the sudden loud chord in the middle of a quiet melody.

Duet Accompaniment

Symphony No. 94

(2nd mvt. theme)

L.H. Position

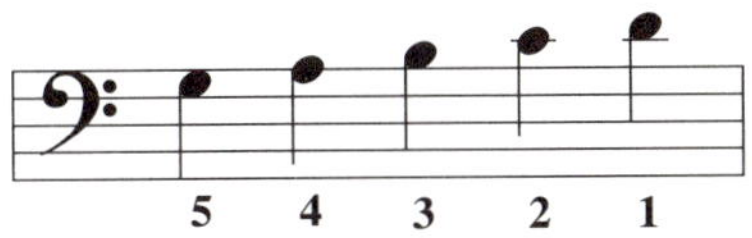

R.H. Positions

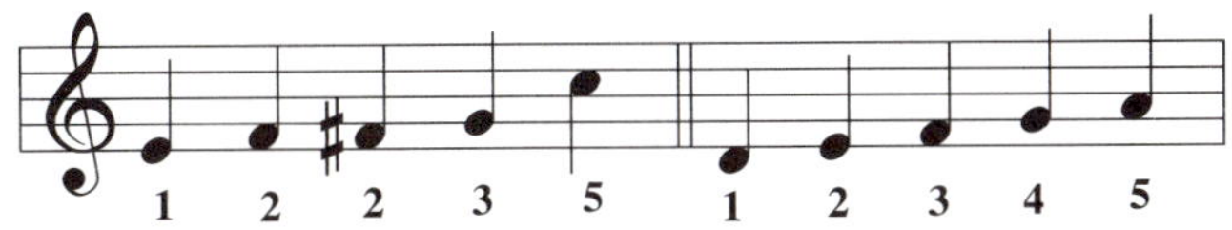

Andante

Franz Joseph Haydn

Johann Ernst Galliard

(GAL-ee-yard) 1687-1749

Galliard was a German composer who spent his career in London. Though his father was a French wig maker, Galliard's talent was squarely in the field of music. He was a very accomplished oboe player, organist, and composer. For a time, Galliard was the oboe player for Handel's opera orchestra.

Galliard also composed many pieces for plays and wrote several operas. Music critics of his day praised his outstanding oboe playing but were divided praising his compositions. One critic was quoted as saying "I never saw more correctness and less originality in any author that I have examined . . ." This melody is from the 3rd movement of his Sonata No. 6 for bassoon or cello, written in 1733.

Unfortunately, no portrait of Galliard is available.

Duet Accompaniment

Sonata No. 6

(3rd mvt. theme)

L.H. Positions

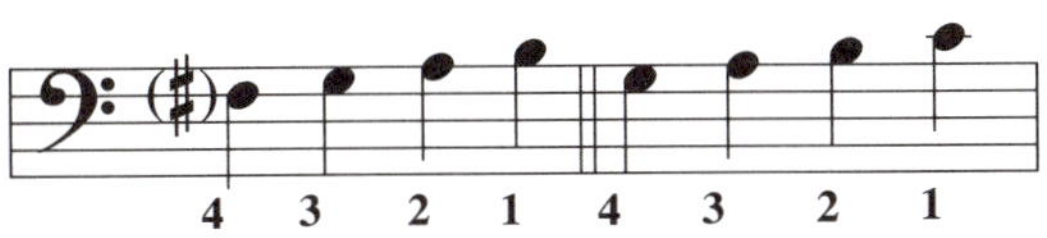

R.H. Position

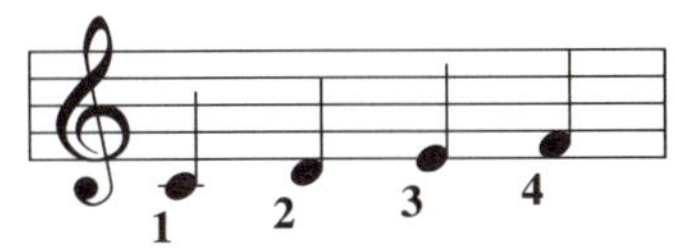

Johann Ernst Galliard

Allegro

Peter Ilyich Tchaikovsky

(chy-KUFF-skee) 1840-1893

Tchaikovsky is arguably the most famous of all Russian composers. He was the son of a mining inspector, and did not really get serious about music as a career until he was in his 20's. After graduating from the St. Petersburg conservatory he made up for lost time by composing at a rapid pace. He wrote music for operas, ballets, orchestras, chamber groups, piano and choirs, and achieved popularity in all these categories.

Tchaikovsky composed the music for the ballet *Sleeping Beauty* in 1889. *Sleeping Beauty* tells the story of a princess who is put to sleep for 100 years by a wicked fairy. She can only be awakened by the kiss of a handsome stranger. Prince Charming has no problem with this. He kisses Sleeping Beauty, she awakens, they get married, and live happily ever after. Tchaikovsky's ballet music is so well written that it is quite often performed on its own by symphony orchestras.

Duet Accompaniment

Sleeping Beauty

L.H. Position

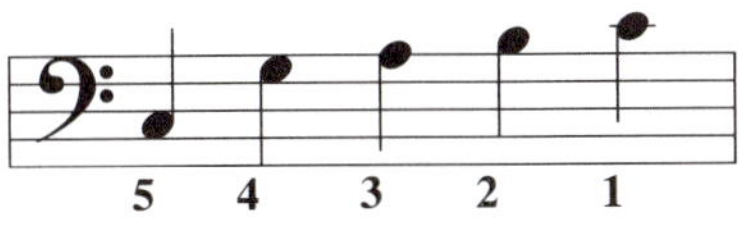

R.H. Position

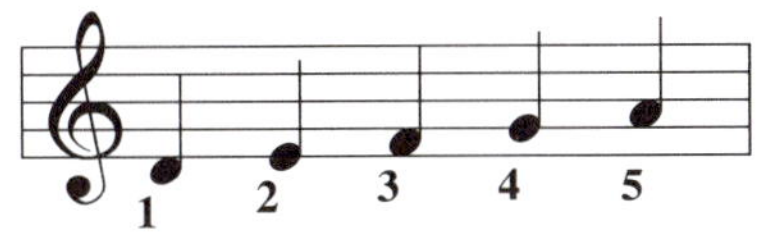

Tempo di Valse

Peter I. Tchaikowsky

Wolfgang Amadeus Mozart

(MOE-tsart) 1756-1791

Mozart's Symphony No. 40 in G minor was written in 1788. It expresses passion and despair. Rhythmically, it is one of the simplest pieces that Mozart ever wrote; the rhythm drives the melody without any surprises.

Mozart made much more effective use of wind instruments in his symphonies than did Haydn. Mozart was particularly fond of the sonorities of the clarinet and the French horn. Despite the appearance of simplicity, Symphony No. 40 is a very expressive work that remains one of the most popular pieces in all of classical music. The style of Mozart's Symphony No. 40 started pushing toward the beginning of the romantic era in music.

Duet Accompaniment

Symphony No. 40

(1st mvt. theme)

Wolfgang Amadeus Mozart

Allegro

LUDWIG VAN BEETHOVEN

(BAY-toe-ven) 1770-1827

One of Beethoven's early music teachers saw the great potential in young Ludwig, and encouraged him to study the works of Bach and to work on keyboard improvisation. Beethoven studied for a while with Haydn and Salieri, and became an accomplished performer on piano and violin. He made a name for himself as a concert pianist in the fashionable salon society in Bonn, Germany. He was one of the first composers who tried to live exclusively as a free-lance artist from the beginning of his career. His reputation soon grew, and in spite of his increasing hearing loss became very successful. Beethoven is recognized as one of the greatest composers who ever lived.

Beethoven's *Piano Sonata No.8* was written between 1797 and 1798, and was subtitled *Pathetique.* In all he wrote 32 piano sonatas.

Duet Accompaniment

Piano Sonata No. 8

(3rd mvt. theme)

L.H. Positions

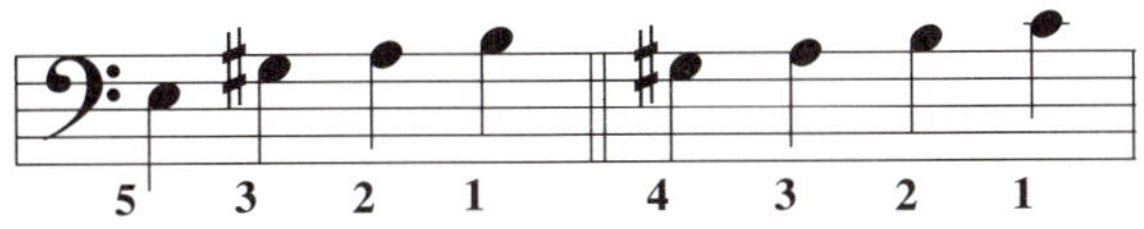

R.H. Positions

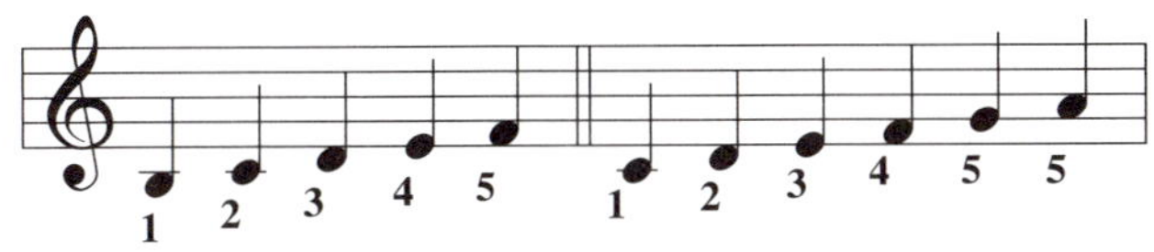

Ludwig van Beethoven

Allegro

Melody

(from *Album for the Young*)

Robert Schumann

Moderato

Robert Schumann

(SHOO-mahn) 1810-1856

Schumann was the youngest of five children. His father was a German bookseller. Schumann composed most of his pieces at the piano, despite his telling his students to begin by thinking their compositions out in their heads. His piano music often is based on clear and simple melodies that are slightly varied throughout the piece.

Melody is the first piece from the collection *Album for the Young, Op. 68,* that Schumann wrote in 1848, after he had written most of his greatest piano works. According to a letter Schumann wrote to a friend, composing these pieces had given him "incredible joy." The *Album for the Young,* said Schumann, embodied the "anticipations and experiences of young people." *Melody* reflects the influence of Bach's music on Schumann. The first seven pieces from his *Album for the Young* were a gift to his daughter Marie for her 7th birthday.

Duet Accompaniment

Musical Terms

used in
Easy Master Themes, Level One

allegro (ah-LEG-grow) Fast; quickly.

andante (ahn-DAHN-tay) Moderately slow.

andantino (ahn-dahn-TEE-noh) A little faster than *andante.*

f Abbreviation of *forte* (FOHR-tay) Loud, strong.

ff Abbreviation of *fortissimo* (fohr-TISS-ee-moh) Very loud.

lento (LEN-toh) Slow.

mf Abbreviation of *mezzo forte* (MET-zoh FOHR-tay) Medium loud; softer than *forte.*

moderato (mah-dur-AH-toh) At a moderate tempo.

mp Abbreviation of *mezzo piano* (MET-zoh pee-YAH-noh) Medium soft.

p Abbreviation of *piano* (pee-YAH-noh) Soft.

tempo di valse (TEMM-poh dih VAHLZ) Literally, in waltz tempo. Speed may range from moderate to fast.